promiscuous

poetry

stanza

laik

stone steps (01 August 2022)

I perch on the landing,
you kneel
on the lowest wrung,
the heat from the concrete
leaks
into the fabric of my skirt.

You are looking up
the stone steps
at me. I unhook my legs
from under my chin.
My back becomes your arch.

My ankle feels the gentle pressure
of your fingers,
you place my feet
shoulder width apart,
Rest them
on the tops of your shoulders.

My back becomes
your bridge.

1 August 2022

I want to watch the hand with your wedding band
Disappear inside me
Until I can only see your wrist.
<><><><><><><><><><><><><><><><><><><><>

I can't wait to lick the tip of each of your fingers.

I point my pelvis at the ceiling
to give you a better view.

<><><><><><><><><><><><><><><><><><><><

I can't hear what anyone is saying today
because I'm trapped inside the moment
you licked yourself out of me.

<><><><><><><><><><><><><><><><><><><><

You make me fear the end of the world.
I think to myself "please don't let me die, universe. Because life feels so good."

<><><><><><><><><><><><><><><><><><><><

The only way I can belong to you is if I want to.
And I really want to.

I love that, after spending the night with me, your wife can't keep her hands off you anymore. It makes me feel like my poetry put something beautiful into the universe.

<><><><><><><><><><><><><><><><><><><><>

I often think about how you fit your entire wedding band inside me.

<><><><><><><><><><><><><><><><><><><><>

If you and I got together for a night, I would make sure you saw everything. I would make sure I pushed your head so your eyes could see, so clearly, where you stopped and I began.

<><><><><><><><><><><><><><><><><><><><>

I feel you, leaking out of me, the next day. I smile. I love it.

<><><><><><><><><><><><><><><><><><><><

You said you like pain so next time, I want to bite your fingers. And drag my fingernails along your spine.

<><><><><><><><><><><><><><><><><><><><>

I want to say and do things that make you clench your jaw.

2 August 2022

The only thing that will cure this ache is your entire fist.

4 August 2022

Beautiful noises.
He tells me I make because
My voice is unique

18 August 2022

You taste yourself
inside of me.
Kneeling,
you say you pray to know
this body.
I laugh and you return
in silent worship.
You unlock
all of my secrets
and all of my dreams.
You listen
to each word.
Between each whimper
you learn
everything
you'll ever need
to love me.

19 August 2022

I sit inside a classroom,
Powerpoint slides by.

I stare at the carpet,
And all I can think of
is sex.

The dormitory across the street
is hollow, under
constant construction,
and beautiful.

The windows are ornate
and blank.

The fluorescence in this room
is stifling.
The bird woman reading off the slides,
word for word,
has stringy hair.
And I wonder what sex she has.
If any.

I feel alone.

I want to shout at her.
There is beauty! Sex! Pleasure!
Have you forgotten, dear child?
There is more to life than
this presentation.
these bills.

I cross my arms
to display my frustration,
to convey my boredom.

I imagine running.
I imagine sliding onto you.
I imagine you being my escape.

I stare at the dormitory across the street.
There is metal. And men. And history being
preserved.

19 August 2022 II

I watch you
while you watch me
with him.

The video is skipped back:
pink, gloss, water.

Your favorite part
is when I growl.

I can dig
Deeper than this.
I can make it more beautiful.
I can make you
never stop watching.

19 August 2022 III

A book rests in your hands. I lace my legs across your lap. Pulling my knees closer to my chest, I form a crescent moon on the couch. My skirt is emerald and the dark hair shows underneath. My heel rests against your thigh. I close my eyes and sleep for an hour. You never turn a single page.

20 August 2022

Hamlet raped me.
We were in high school.
I didn't speak up.
I learned to stay silent.
Now I put Hamlet
On my bookshelf
And I think of him
As he covers dust
And that's his little space
Left over in my life.
And that's alright.

20 August 2022 II

I kiss the eye
of your dominant palm.
You take a deep breath
and groan.
I study each callous
like a feather.
Your hand is my world.
The tip of each finger
slips passed my lips.
The purple pool
under your thumb
disappears.
There,
and not there.
Your paw clutches

my jaw,
another sharp instinct.
I listen. I follow.

Fingerprints
Veins
Mini hairs
Freckles
Rings

21 August 2022

The next morning,
I discover faint evidence of you.
Marking my black hoodie.
I'm standing in line at the store
While I'm buying a gallon of milk.
It makes me smile.

21 August 2022 II

Your eyes
track me.
Study
every note
while I'm naked
and shivering.
They scan
and

predict.
But the muscles of my thighs
begin to burn.
I break
your point of contact.
The separation
makes you search.
I rest on my back,
and re-open.
Your heavy brow
relaxes.
The drama is only
milliseconds.
Your eyes could be
a play:
first act, second,
and
Curtains.

22 August 2022

I love being workshopped.
A painting or sculpture.
But only if I trust the person
will I listen.

22 August 2022 II

I dream about your wife.
How can I fantasize
About a person I've never met
Or spoken to?
Because
Your love pours out of you
I suppose.

22 August 2022 III

Context is important.
That's why I include dates
as poem titles.
Could the same poem
have been written on
22 August 1981?
Does a date
Create a picture
In your mind
Of a snapshot in your existence
Or an event
That changed your life?

22 August 2022 IIII

Hamlet raped me
when I was 14.

So tell me
why do I keep Hamlet on my bookshelf?

Is it the need
to manufacture
meaning?

I've moved
a hundred times
and sold my library
thrice.

So tell me, if Hamlet raped me
when I was 14,
and he was 16,
why do I carry Hamlet
from house to house?

Considering,
if I created Utopia,
my only crime would be rape.

But still
I've made
a thousand excuses:
a miscommunication.

But my eyes stayed squeezed shut.
I slammed my teeth together,
never made a sound.

Does that sound like
consent
to you?

I spent a decade
convincing myself
I asked for it.

Because I wrote him
a Stargram
during intermission.

Because I loved
his brooding portrayal of the doomed prince.

I was a virgin.

And the consequences
were worse than pain.
I told no one.

The girl who asked her mother, eagerly,
to explain penetration, when she was 10.

She learned
numb.

The generous spectrum
of sex

erased,

like stealing colors
from the rainbow.

I had to take newspaper
with my rapist
for a year.
His girlfriend was my editor
and she hated me.

The two of them got cancer young,
and their lives were
forever weaved.

So tell me why
I keep Hamlet
on my bookshelf?
Why do I move him
from place to place,
inside a book I never open?

Hamlet,
I'd forgive you for murder
but I'll never forgive your rape.

No matter what you make yourself.

Even as I write
I want to believe
it wasn't in violation.
It was an honest mistake.

But that isn't true.
You filled sex
with a river of fear.
You made me hate kissing.

When I was 13,
Steven and I used to sneak off
just to kiss.

One night,
against the post office.

Steven lifted me up.
I wrapped my legs around his waist.

Under the bed
at Mika's party,
we kissed for hours.
Feet shuffled by our faces.

He never did the vile shit you did.
He had ample opportunity.
It wasn't a mistake.

Is it all because
I made Hamlet
into my God?

23 August 2022

I picture my mouth
on the woman you love.

It makes me long for her body.

How can I feel this way
about a person I've never met
or spoken to?

Perhaps,

it is because

love
pours
out of you
and into me.

23 August 2022 II

I brand you.
With my real name.
You are one of the few
to learn it.
I don't want you ever to forget.

24 August 2022

I've never met a girl who loves to look
as much as you.
It is because I memorize.
I hit every note.
I let you see every drop.
I hide nothing.
Would you like
to come in my mouth?
I make you speak.
I cling to every word.
I want you to ask yourself,
who am I?

25 August 2022

You lift my sweatshirt,
put your ear to my back.

Outline the hips
of the caryatid.

My vertebrae,
the column,
along which,
our hands clutch
like ivy.

The pillar
test the tension
between you
and me.

What do I hold on my shoulders?

"Bracing is reinforcement. One form is cross bracing which features two members organized in an X shape so that one deals with tension and the other with compression."

-belfry
-canopy
-"a caryatid is a sculptural column in the form of a woman"
-curvilinear

26 August 2022

Am I the lost place

or the radio?

You lift my sweatshirt,

put your ear against my back,

listen to each vertebrae.

The radio illuminates,

the lost-place haunts.

26 August 2022 II

I'm your receiver
Artifacting transmissions
From the world unseen.

26 August 2022 III

You finger my spine
Tracing each of the notches
I, Caryatid

26 August 2022 IIII

If we never come like this again
My only dream is that
You always remember
What I feel like

27 August 2022

I hate the need
in my eyes
while I scream
for you.
But I long
that you
look back,
and watch
the joy enter
from you, to me.

28 August 2022

I lift up
so that
when you plunge,
you fall out of me,

It's a step in a dance, a stroke of bright feathers.

I like you to know

the changing topography,
inside me.

You glimpse
in the pause:

Your shape
leaves an imprint.

30 August 2022

A poet studies the invisible.

This is your body,
filled with unseen.

She shines light in your ears,
counts your pulse,
listens to your lungs,
traces each bone.

She reports her findings.

She does this
so she'll feel less alone.

30 August 2022 II

Confess awful things
you think
you've done.
I'll tell you,
They are awful.
But I understand.

30 August 2022 III

We shower together
So that you keep me safe.
It isn't a fantasy.
It is for your disabled friend
In this disabled body
That seeks to be pleasured by you.
We wash each other's bodies
To cleanse everything that we bring.

31 August 2022

Don't rush to find your way back
into me.
Please.
Take your time in circles.

01 September 2022

Your tangled body
is my study.

I breathe light in your ear,
obey your throat as you swallow.

I count the routes your heart wants to take.
I percuss the hollow.

I press my fingers to
cross sect the invisible.

Your pupils
track my deliberate hands.
Your grip finds mine
like granite.

I stop collecting data.

I absorb the river
from the nucleus
where I am clenched around you.

02 September 2022

52 hours, you were mine.
I refused an epidural.
Refused
to set foot in a hospital.

52 hours,
divided into contractions,
I locked wolf eyes with yours,
the only thing
keeping me from falling
off the earth.

The pain would wake me from sleep
with a moan. There, you perched.

It would be the last time it was ever
just
us.

03 September 2022

My longing to have you
in me,
to pin you
to the bed,
yawns wide,
stretching down my anterior,
reaching into my core
and thrusting me out of sleep.
That is how deeply I want you.
There is no line between need and want.
There is only the ache of awaiting you.

03 September 2022 II

I was cast as a prostitute at 17.
In Les Mis, on stage,
they painted a rainbow on my sternum
Brown and white
every audience member
complimented my realistic cleavage

They decked me in a blue dress that
Exposed the ridgeline of my clavicles.

At 21 I joined a sorority.
In writing class you loved that part of me.
Sorostitute.

My favorite class was rural sociology.

I met you, and we made eye contact
backstage, or in the auditorium signing autographs.

03 September 2022 III

The ivy draped on
the tree looks like a woman.
And I think of you.

04 September 2022

You stand before a woman. She offers you a mask. "Put this on, please."

She waits for you to secure it over your mouth and nose, only your eyes visible above the fabric. Then she takes a step toward you, reaching to lift your shirt. You let her.

She sighs and looks you straight in the eyes."If you want to sleep with me, you must shower with me first."

You nod. "Of course."

Her eyes flicker. You see that she'd been ready for you to protest. This hardened creature. Even though you let her remove your belt and pants next, she continues on her rehearsed script, "Your microorganisms have killed many of us. And I must survive."

After the shower, she is glistens and shivers. Her jaw clatters with cold. She looks up and down your naked form as you dry off.

"Can you hug me?" She asks.

"Of course," and you wrap her in your arms. She doesn't feel as cold but you feel her muscles quake.

Your hands can reach almost all the way around her. After a while, the spasm in her spine quiets. A tendril of her breath, swirls around your ear. She rests her cheek against your neck. Her toes curl around your calf. "My feet are still freezing."

04 September 2022 II

I allow myself 30 minutes
to sink into bitterness.

My cheekbones burn
at you denying me what I wanted.

Hatred is like sugar.

But before the timer is up,
my clutched anger breaks

into understanding.

I see your mistake:
you're not a monster.
I tried to tell you:
I like you, stupid.

When I pout,
I call people names,
like a child.

04 September 2022 III

since we fuck for art
(and making art is work)

every emotion of falling in love
is our canvas.

But each arrow can be captured midair
and repurposed into deeper understanding,

Artistic friendship.

Think about it:

If you're not allowed to say "I love you"
imagine all the ways you'll show it.

Perhaps you will become it

and walk around pouring it into other people.

05 September 2022

Movie subtitles.
Are the code that will decode
everything for us.

05 September 2022 II

We are both artists
You fuck me on film
I let you take photos of me
Post coitus
It seems like a fair trade.
I imagine you using me for cachet telling people you're working in sex with no other details given
That makes me smile.
And I like when you get your hair out of your face so I can see it.

05 September 2022 III

The toddler has newspaper ink
on their feet. They snot and use accessory muscles. Balloons
scattered across the living room floor.

This is the ordinary scene the day following our first (not last)
threesome
I feel goofy like a child.

We color on the newspaper with markers.
I draw outlines of blue coffee mugs.
I highlight letters in red and ask them to point.

A headline for a story reads "Creating a Refuge In the
Romantic."

05 September 2022 IIII

I watch your reflection over my shoulder,
your hair disarrayed.

I've already exhausted you
between round one
and round two.

I lean on the counter with my pants off.

I color my eyes in with blue.

You listen to my story of,
The ghost of
3am,
I left no trace,
but my leopard thong on his floor.

I grin ear to ear, delighted

at the easy flow of my words.

You point the lens at my back as I laugh.

05 September 2022 V

You're a little more than half erect.
And yet,
you make me come.
Twice.
Your real name escapes, a shout.
You learn the rhythm of me.
After practice,
you master it.
Finally I,
after practice,
unhook my tongue,
stop my selective mutism,
and command you
on exactly how.

06 September 2022

When you lift my hips off the mattress
and look down on me like that,
I get chills.
Because I know
you look down on no one.
You show me: we could be any one.
You cherish what is called ugly,
as much as what is called beautiful.
You reach into my Monday solitude,
and thrust me off autopilot,
so that I'm talking to this houseless man
about his daughter
and clean sheets
and water,
standing on the concrete outside CVS,
handing him what I had,
irritated
I couldn't give him
more.

07 September 2022

I feel ill with jealousy,
a desire for possession
Crushing me to the bed
on my face.
I want you to be mine forever.

Before I snap into realization that the emotion
is poison
And ownership is a myth
I imagine you with a woman prettier than me
and it makes me ill.

But then
I watch our content together
And it is beautiful
And it is bigger than us
And you and I will always be free in our hearts

08 September 2022

I wear a green dress and black heels
It's 7am and the contractors are filling up their trucks
I know I look better than coffee
And everyone is still half asleep
And horny
I lean over as far as I can
To give all of them a show
Because people are tired and beat down

08 September 2022 II

I could sleep with anyone
But I choose you.
Because the way my son
looks up to his father.

08 September 2022 III

I can't believe
you think I'm worth all this trouble.
I flinch when you talk,
waiting for you to bail.
To lose your faith in me.

I am disabled-inspiration porn. Hot-girl syndrome.
Baby-of-the-family syndrome.

I can't believe you would
jump through as many hoops as this.
I never knew
I'd always had the hoops
but I gave everyone else a "pass"
even if they weren't man enough to reach
the top wrung.

08 September 2022 IIII

How to become a sex goddess

You ask for a story about me. You know my true name. Among the few.
Hand in palm. Ears and eyes fixed on me.
There's a reason cool boys always liked stories of me as a girl.
Like the pink bunny costume. We'll get to that.

I swear I wasn't a totally neglected child.
I played a lot by myself,
I hung out in trees, imagined a palace, with boardwalks connecting the canopies.
I was a naive child. I didn't understand why I couldn't make my hand into a uniform mud print, or squat down and pee on the dirt pile in the front yard. Where all the neighbors could see.

I discovered self pleasure, against a metal pole, at recess in grade school. And thought, when I did it, at home against the door, the pleasure was so amazing, I was certain I was going to hell.

And then I grew up and things got worse: I got pretty. Really pretty. Pretty enough that my brother made comments. In a factual way.

I had an odd face. So I wasn't a hot popular girl. I was a hot loner girl, the girl who liked writing and math. Two boys agreed to be my dates to Homecoming. Another carved my initials in his arm with a knife. I made friends just fine. They didn't last, but I didn't understand that they were supposed to.

I slept with Aaron when I was 16. I kept my eyes closed the entire time. I didn't know how to break up with Aaron, so I slept with Derek at 18. Aaron's best friend passed me jogging at the pond. He yelled "Slut!"

I forgot to mention: during all of this I got diabetes. When I was 14. And was raped in the same year. And oh, boy, did I manage to bury that deep.

So, the wake-up from that? The flip of the page from Acknowledgements to Chapter 1? The funeral for that body?

It's a door that was locked. It's like opening the door, after

finally figuring out the key.

About the Author

stanzalaik.square.site

www.ingramcontent.com/pod-product-compliance
Lightning Source LLC
LaVergne TN
LVHW052110160826
845678LV00015B/3468

9798371790217